LAST MOMENTS

The Dark Shadows of Protest in Iran

HIRBOD HUMAN

2024

Book edited by **Edward Wall**
Development edits by **Siamak S. Karimi**
Cover design by **Hirbod Human**

2026 Next Generation Indie Book Awards Finalist
Regional (Fiction)

First printing

Contents

To the valiant women and men of Iran, whose sacrifices in the name of freedom illuminate the struggle against tyranny and injustice. In the face of tyranny, the bravest act is to stand up and speak the truth, even when the world chooses to remain silent.

History will not forget you.

Introduction

The duty of an artist extends beyond creating works of art; it involves documenting the harsh truths of their time for those unaware of these realities, and for future generations. Through this act an artist might hope to prevent the recurrence of human atrocities. Throughout history, artists, especially writers, have served as truthful narrators of their era. Great writers have played this role, preserving the essence of their historical context through their work.

This collection of six stories narrates the fate of people who stood up against oppression and demanded their rights. As an Iranian, I have written these stories to depict the harsh realities of life under the Islamic Republic of Iran. In countries controlled by ideological and totalitarian regimes, where the simple act of protest can cost people their well-being and even their lives. Having fled such inequalities myself, I now live in the United States. I see those who escape the wrath of political and religious tyrants as soldiers running for help to save those still in the grip of tyranny.

I was born in 1979, the year the Shah fell, and a brutal revolution handed control of the state to the most extreme, violent, and deceitful factions of society. Over four decades of international silence allowed me and others like me to become children of war, bullets, fire, prison, torture, and execution.

These stories are drawn from my personal

experiences and hours of interviews with victims of human-rights violations in Iran; prisoners, their families, soldiers, torturers, and politicians who have realized the extent of their crimes and are now seeking to prevent these atrocities from continuing. Although the names and details in these stories are fictional, the situations they depict are not. Every word reflects the bitter moments left from the sweetness of life for those who either perished or lived on, broken and scarred.

These narratives shine a light on men and women who, beyond their political inclinations, sought only freedom and equality—values the world, especially the Western world, proclaims as fundamental human rights. These stories reveal the lives of children who lost their parents in the most brutal ways, often without even a grave to mourn over. These are the tales of survivors of terror and despair.

I have written these stories so that history does not forget these brave individuals—girls and boys, men and women. These accounts aim to prevent politicians from using the rhetoric of freedom while millions are sacrificed for trying to exercise their fundamental rights. My hope is to remind those who champion freedom not to compromise with history's tyrants and to enlighten future generations on how easily valuable lives are sacrificed for political greed and ambition to wield power.

This collection is a testament to those who have suffered and a call to remember and honor their struggles. It is a simple yet profound plea for justice, meant to resonate deeply and inspire action against the atrocities that continue to plague our world.

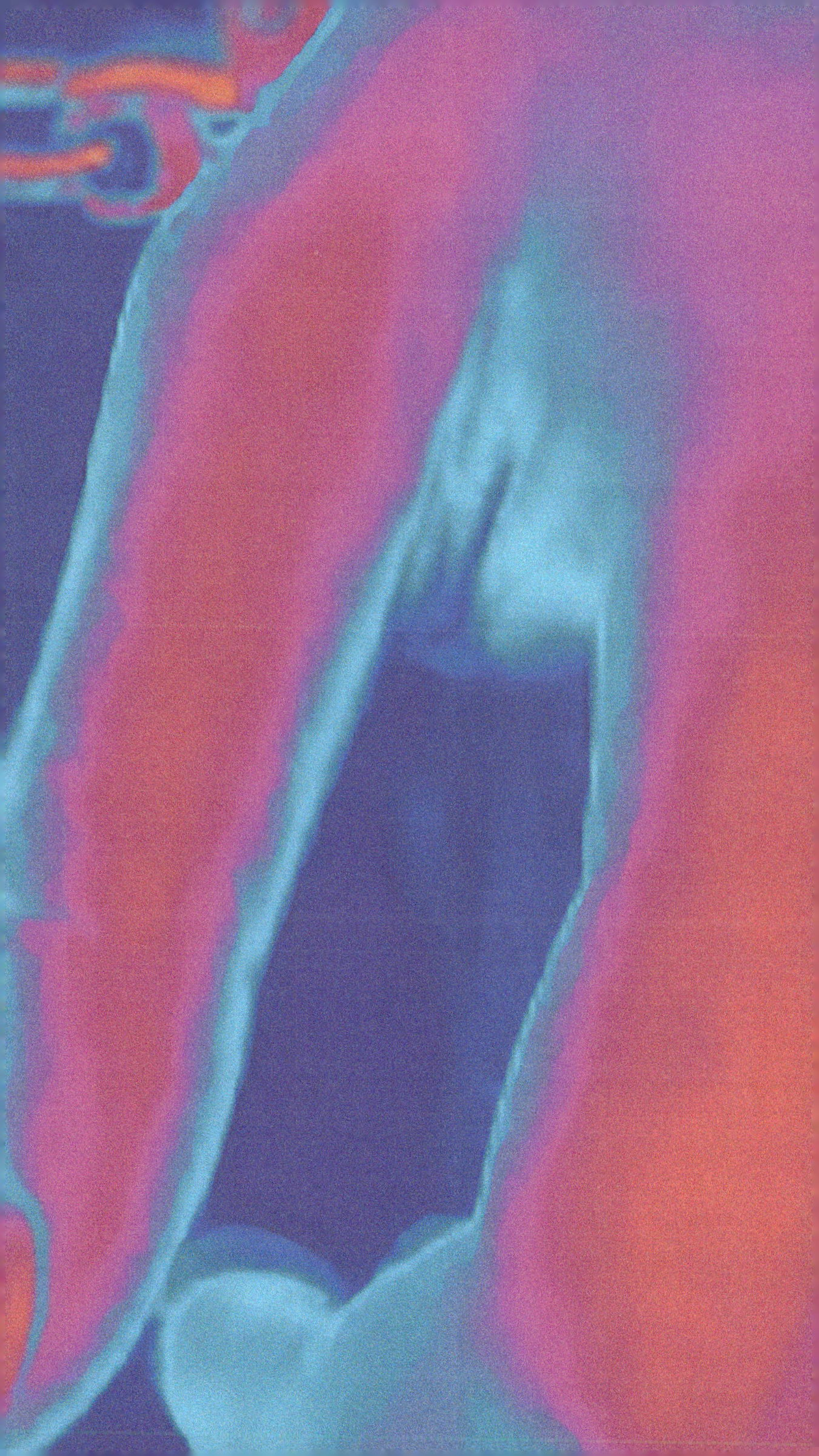

Airport

A dirty, small two-by-two-meter room. A black metal chair in one corner, an old metal table carved up with names, dates, and nervous scribbles in another. On the wall, an old analog clock with a white face and cloudy glass showed 3:05. Above the closed door, a CCTV camera pointed at the chair, a small red light glowing underneath.

The fluorescent light was bothering her. She had always hated those, and now she could hear its buzzing sound. Her mind was blank. With her palms pressed together and her arms hugging her knees she whispered a song. It was an old song, known off by heart by every child, but now she couldn't remember the words. Sometimes, when her voice got lost in the emptiness of her mind, she would hum the melody.

The door handle swung down forcefully, and the door opened a crack, making her jump. She could hear her heart racing and tried to take a deep breath but gasped for air. Whoever had opened the door was making no move to enter. Her mind latched on to the sounds that filtered through the small gap. She could hear the echo of the floor cleaner's brushes turning and scrubbing but not people's voices. From this she concluded that the airport was now closed. She could hear the echo of the floor cleaner's brushes turning and scrubbing but not the people's voices. The door stayed cracked, the door handle still facing down towards the ground. After what felt like an eternity, she heard a deep male voice, loud, close by, from just the other side of the door, calling loudly.

"Any news Fallah? Have they arrived?" He released the door handle and took a couple of steps away from the door. "Did you contact them? What are you doing?" he demanded. She heard the sound of rushed footsteps, and a new voice, slightly muffled, replied, "The car has arrived, sir. They said they are doing some coordination." The door slammed shut, and the first voice yelled again, "Fallah!"

"Yes, Captain?"

"Go get blindfolds from them. Hurry up!"

"Sir, yes, sir," Fallah answered.

The door opened fully now, and a man in his forties, wearing a dark green Iranian

Revolutionary Guard's uniform with a captain's badge, entered the room. She looked up at him, at his obscene smile. He stepped towards her. "Up," he snapped, gesturing with his hand. She stood in front of him. He was breathing heavily, and she had to fight to suppress her reaction to the smell of it. He was a head taller than her. He slapped her zip-tied hands. "Up," he repeated, and she raised them, flinching as he cut the restraints with a large pair of scissors, sending pieces of plastic flying across the room. "Turn around," he ordered, cutting her off before she could speak. "Your situation doesn't concern me. I have a job to do. Turn around." She followed his orders, trembling as she faced the wall. "Hands behind your back." She placed her pale, cold hands against her spine, whimpering softly as the captain pulled them up with force. He pulled out another zip tie from his pocket and bound her hands again, the plastic tugging at her skin. "Don't move." He said that and took a couple of steps back, poked his head out of the door, and called, "Fallah!"

A young boy with a shaved head delivered the blindfold.

"Here you are, sir. The lady interrogator's gone to the bathroom." The captain took the blindfold, ignoring him, and ordered him to get her documents and belongings. "Her mother is tearing herself apart," the young soldier replied quietly. The captain cut him off.

"Mind your business and go get her stuff!" he roared.

When the soldier left, the captain shut the door, stepped toward her, and stood behind her, facing the wall. As he moved his hands to cover her eyes, she flinched at the touch of the fabric.

"Are you scared? God knows when you'll be able to see again." He grinned as he taunted her. His words shivered down her spine.

Tears pooled in her eyes, though they had nowhere to run. He pressed on her shoulder roughly, turning her around to face him. Inches apart, she could feel his breath on her skin. Her knees shook, growing weaker as the fear intensified, and she struggled to resist the natural reaction to urinate. Her ears rang, and cold sweat covered her forehead. She desperately wanted to call out for her mother but couldn't. Her brain was unable to command her mouth.

The door opened, and the captain's bulk shifted away from her as he turned to look. She heard Fallah's voice:

"I have her belongings, sir."

"Take them to the car and tell the interrogator to wait in the lobby. I'll call her," the captain replied.

"Yes, sir," the young soldier said quietly and closed the door.

The captain stared at her lips, his head moving sideways back and forth, like a hungry hyena watching its prey. She imagined his hand on her back, moving around as if searching her body. She shuddered and curled into herself like a withered flower. "Do you have anything on you?" he asked, and she imagined him touching her with both hands. She started crying quietly, her body shivering, her knees shaking.

"Are you crying? Are you guilty? Didn't you say there's been a mistake?" He pressed and touched her body hard with his fingers and palms, like a rubbing felt. "If you were innocent, you would have stayed in your homeland. You must be guilty if you want to escape," he murmured in her ear, his body touching hers.

Suddenly, the door flew open and hit the wall, squeaking loudly.

"I'm Rahmani," a woman said, entering the room. The captain took a step back, though his body was still touching hers.

"She's yours. Her papers and belongings were sent to the car. Give the transfer papers to Fallah," he snarled, skulking away. "You might want to take her to the bathroom first," he added with an evil smile, drying his wet hand with a napkin from his pocket.

Prison

It was five in the morning. In the corner of a damp, cold, and dark solitary cell by the door, a skinny twenty-seven or twenty-eight-year-old man was lying on the floor on his left side, hugging his knees like a fetus in its mother's womb. His eyes looked like two lines in his punched, slapped and swollen face. He was whimpering, with a weak smile on his chapped and bruised lips. It looked like he was enduring a lot of pain to keep this smile, and the wider it was, the deeper his frown became.

He seemed to be looking at someone, but

there was only a broken, stinky toilet a meter in front of him, and behind it, a wall. His legs could have passed the toilet bowl if he'd straightened them. The cell was only five feet by eight feet, with a high ceiling and no windows—a heavy metal door with a small shoe-box-sized sliding door, which, of course, was closed. He could hear a distant moaning and thought to himself, "His moaning is louder than mine, which means his condition is better than mine," and smiled. He was happy for the other man and started talking to him and comforting him. "Don't be afraid. It is all like a bad dream. It will all go away. We are here together."

A metal lock shunted open somewhere far off, its weight echoing down the hallway. He heard the footsteps that always followed and asked himself, "How many this time?" With quivering legs, he smiled, and his frown deepened. The pain was still there. The footsteps got closer. He thought, "Two people? No, three? No, there are more. Maybe four people." The footsteps got closer. The distant moaning voice had completely stopped. "They're coming for me." He had a strange feeling in his body. He could smell the end, the smell of death, relief from the pain. Whenever he thought about freedom, the pain subsided, but the quivers grew. He couldn't control them, and it bothered him. The footsteps were closer. Now his stomach and any part of his body that had been beaten over the last couple of weeks quivered. The footsteps stopped by the cell, but someone else was still coming, walking heavily, wearing slippers and dragging his feet on the floor. He knew these footsteps. His feeling was right. Freedom was close.

A drawling voice said, "Bring him out." The small sliding door, like a hatch where food comes in, though no food had ever come in for him, opened, and light from the hallway lifted the shadows. The small door closed again, but his back was to the door, so he didn't see any of it. Then, with the sound of the lock, the cell door opened, and a man at the door said, "He's still on the floor." The farther voice, which was clearer now, and closer, asked, "Is he conscious?" A pair of legs stepped into his line of vision: brown uniform pants. A face loomed down over him, that of a young man with lazy eyes and a dark curly beard, sweat on the collar of a light blue shirt.

"Yes sir, I think he's awake."

"Bring him outside." He had a familiar accent, but the young man couldn't place it. Two men entered the room and lifted him by his shoulders like a saddlebag, his body still shaking, the legs of his pants stuck to his skin, heavy with urine. One of them told the other, "Watch out, he's najis." The other didn't respond. They dragged him to the doorway. The man who opened the door moved a few steps back, and and the fat mullah, massive in height as well as girth, dressed in religious attire without a turban, with his metal glasses and a short trimmed beard, said, "Lift his head." The man holding him did what he was told. Behind the young man's swollen eyelids, his eyeballs were only two bloody red slashes. The torture had damaged his vision, causing him to see everything in a blurred, reddish haze, with the mullah as the centerpiece of this painful image. He still had the smile on his lips, and it was with only a near-superhuman effort that he was keeping it there. With knees bent, he was unable to stand.

The mullah said nicely with a smile, "Thank God you are doing well, even smiling. Seems like you're having a good time here, Mr. Arman. You've just shrunk a bit. When you arrived, you were so tall we had to look up in the sky to see you. Now you are shorter and better behaved." Picking up the corners of his robe, he continued, "I've also heard that you haven't written your death wish. We've prepared everything for you to do it, but you didn't want to. Don't worry. I will personally tell your mother you are okay and regret everything."

Arman stopped shaking after hearing this, though the name felt distant and unfamiliar, as if it belonged to someone else. "Take him quickly and get him cleaned up. Give him some water also," the mullah ordered. "It's almost sunrise." The man replied, "Yes, sir." The mullah moved a few steps back, and the two men dragged Arman away. The third man pulled out his radio and spoke into it. "Are the other five ready?" Someone at the other end responded, "Yes."

Someone at the other end said, "Yes, they are."

"Do you need six soldiers?"

"Of course six. Why are you asking nonsense, Ahmad?"

The soldier Ahmad took Arman roughly by the arm. There was no need for force: Arman went along pliantly, much like a trusting child. Though too weak to even consider resistance he still wore his faint smile. They moved in procession down hallways, through doors, until they arrived in a big room that looked like a medical exam room. A man wearing a white lab coat moved aside as they entered. They put Arman on a chair and the man, pointing to a metal water pitcher and cup on the table behind him, told one of them, "Baghi, give him some water." Baghi filled the cup with some iced water and walked towards Arman. The other two stood on both sides of him, and one of them kept him from falling by holding his shoulder. The man in the white coat took a prefilled syringe from the table, came towards Arman and asked, "Still no death wish? What type of dying is this?" Then he told Baghi, "Splash some cold water on his face and the back of his neck to wake him up," and to the other man, "Hold his hand." Then he told Arman, "Don't move. I don't want the needle to break in your arm and kill you, to have your death on my conscience. This drug is going to relax you and make you feel better." Then he asked him, "Are you scared?" This made Arman's quivers get worse. He said, "Your shivers will also go away." He signaled the two men. Baghi and the other man held Arman's arms tight, pulled his right sleeve up, and the doctor poked Arman's right arm with the needle and injected the drug. Then he told Baghi, "Give him some water."

Arman's eyes were wider. The doctor was right. The shivers were slowing down. He could breathe now, and for the first time in a long time, he took a half-deep breath; but the smile on his face was gone. The doctor stood in front of him, with the syringe in his hand and asked, "Any death wishes that you want me to write down? Not much time left." Arman, who was numb, didn't say anything and just looked at him. The doctor told one of the men, "Wait for ten minutes so he will feel better. Then take him. Not much left until sunrise." Then he took his lab coat off. He was wearing the same blue shirt and brown pants as the other man. He left the room.

It was 6:05 in the morning. Five blindfolded prisoners with their hands tied behind them were lined up beside the door in the small yard, Six uniformed soldiers and six non-military government officials, likely from judicial or other government divisions, surrounded them. The non-army men were talking quietly and sometimes pointing at the prisoners who were waiting to be executed. One of them was crying. Another was whispering to himself, maybe a prayer or his ashhad—his death verse. One was quiet, the youngest one. The oldest man said quietly but firmly with a Kurdish accent, "Do not fear. Be brave, victory is ours." The soldiers were not breathing, like they were the ones who were going to be executed.

They brought Arman from the end of the hallway. He looked better and his legs were straight, but two men were still holding his arms. When he got closer to the small yard door, he looked up. At the end of the yard, there was a wall pointed at by two big spotlights, as though it was a stage. The sudden brightness was shocking, an affront to the dawn, whose approach could be felt in the dewy morning air, if not yet seen. The wall had been wounded by thousands of bullets. Under the wall, the ground was covered with a two-meter-wide layer of old blood like a dark cloud. As soon as they arrived at the door, the same man who opened Arman's cell door came towards him from the group of non-army men. The others stopped talking and one of them used his radio and said something like, "He's here." It was still dark, but you could feel the sun. It was back there somewhere and wanted to show up. Would he feel the warmth of its touch one last time? They blindfolded his eyes. Baghi told him, "It's time you stand on your own feet." The older prisoner heard him and yelled with a strong Kurdish accent, "Do not fear! Die like a man! Victory is with us!"

The soldiers jumped at his voice. The non-army man beside him elbowed him in the stomach, saying, "Shut up! You keep saying this nonsense with this annoying voice even on death row. Half an hour ago you were crying and begging us to have mercy on you because of your young children." At these words the man, who was now curled up in pain, started crying. All five of them were quietly crying, and whispering to themselves, but Arman was calm and numb.

The mullah and two men arrived in the yard from another passage. The sunlight was appearing in the blackness of the morning. Te soldiers took the five prisoners to where the dusty ground was stained black and stood them in a row, backs to the wall, half a meter apart from each other. The third spot from the left was empty. The same man who opened Arman's cell door looked at the mullah, who was standing with the doctor and a bald man in a suit carrying some files. The doctor signaled and they took Arman to the empty spot. Beside him on one side was the older prisoner, and on the other side, the youngest one. The older prisoner was whispering his death verse and the younger one was singing his mother's lullaby quietly. The doctor came towards Arman and said, "Goodbye, Mr. Arman. Hope to see you again," and laughed.

Arman was numb but standing on his feet.

The air smelled like iron. The thick sponge mat under his feet was partly dry and partly thick and moist. Time was passing strangely. He remembered all his childhood, and at the same time he remembered nothing about it. It was like his brain wanted to show him whatever he'd seen, heard, or felt throughout his life in his last moments. He felt full of grace. He hadn't felt like this for weeks, maybe months or years even. He couldn't tell if it had been seconds or minutes since he'd been standing there. He could hear the voices but didn't understand them. They were meaningless sounds to him. But one voice among them had meaning. He knew this one. Suddenly, the frightening sound of gunfire, the smell of ammunition in the front and dust in the back. His body was hot. His knees bent.

First, his knees buckled, and then his face lay on the warm and wet mat, becoming one with it. He thought to himself: "so this is how you die? It isn't that hard." He could feel the blood under his face and body. The warm blood hugged him like kind, warm arms.

The gunfire stopped. He could hear footsteps now. A gunshot. He thought to himself, "Execution shot." A second gunshot. The third one sounded right in his brain. And then two more, but he could still hear it? He asked himself, "Am I dead? Doesn't your perception die with you? I'm free. I miss my mother so much. I'm sure she will come with my father to greet me. How about Maryam?" The thought of her sent an electric wave through his body.

He heard the doctor's voice in his ear, "You are not dead? Your time isn't up. You are not supposed to go yet. Where do you want to go? Stay with us, you brave Mr. Arman. We still have a lot to do with you." Then he told the non-army men to pick him up. Arman had wet himself. His face and body were bloody, but not with his blood. It was the young and the older man's blood. They picked him up. His body was very weak again, but he was aware of his surroundings now and heard the voices. The doctor said, "Take him to his cell. We will chat again tomorrow." He turned to Arman and said, "Finding and bringing you here wasn't easy, and letting you go won't be either." Then he turned towards the mullah.

Family

"Rojan my daughter, where are you going? You are gonna deliver any day now and it's dangerous to travel. Listen to me, my love. His father is there, his brother is there. They called and said he was being released. They've figured my son is innocent. Where do you wanna go? Come sit for a second. It's not good for the baby, just look at these two innocent souls crying so badly. They are gonna come. It's a man's place. Where are you going, this far into your pregnancy?" Rojan, out of breath with her nine-month pregnant belly, was absentmindedly pulling robes and scarves from the old closet and shoving them into a dark blue duffle bag in her hand.

The old woman held her hand and said, "My dear, my baby, you don't need this many scarves. You just took five. I'm telling you, you are not well. Come sit, honey. Let me get you some iced sherbet with mint extract. You'll feel better. And I will go with you. Am I not his mother? He's my child. You are too. I want to go with you. We'll go together. Come have a seat."

Rojan broke into tears with her puffy eyes and said, "I know he's not released. I know something is going on. I feel it. They haven't released my Atta. My Atta is anxious. I can feel it. My baby in my womb can feel it. It's been like a rock and hasn't moved since this sunrise. I have to go. I have to go myself. My Atta is anxious." The mother stroked Rojan's long and curly black hair with her hand, sat her down by the pillow beside the closet and sat next to her. Then turned toward a nine-year-old boy and six-year-old girl, who were standing at the door and crying, and told them, "Enough. Why are you two crying? Your dad is doing fine. He's released and on his way home. Stop crying. Don't you see how your very pregnant mom doesn't feel well? Tahmooress dear, go make your mom a sherbet. Get some mint extract and rose water from the pantry and add to it."

The boy ran out quickly and the grandmother yelled, "Don't forget to put ice in it!" She turned to the young girl and with her sweet Kurdish accent said, "Come here, don't cry, my baby Kazhalak. Come rub your mommy's shoulders, the same way she rubs mine." And told Rojan, "Her little hands have the same healing power as yours, my beautiful girl; they are like your hands. Why are you letting bad thoughts into your heart? They are gonna call. Maybe there's been some paperwork. Maybe he's had some problems. Two grown men have gone after him. They will come. They will update us. They've taken sweets with them to celebrate. They will bring him. Good news is on its way but good news takes longer to arrive, my dear."

The young girl was rubbing her mom's shoulders with her little hands and the pregnant mother with her big belly was sitting miserably on the floor, opening her legs so her belly would fit between her legs and her body. The grandmother got up, with pain, holding her knees, went to the doorway and yelled, "Tahmooress, where's the sherbet? Your mom doesn't feel well. Bring the sherbet already." The young boy arrived at the door in a hurry and the grandmother pointed at him and said, "Go, baby. Go give it to your mother to make her feel better. Rub your mother's arms and legs. You're your mother's man now."

Tahmooress sat beside his mother, gave the sherbet to her, and started rubbing her calf. Rojan took a sip of the sherbet held in her left hand and with her other hand stroked Kajal's little hands, who was rubbing her shoulders, and then pressed Tahmooress's hands on her calf. She was very stressed. Something inside her, other than her nine-month-old baby, was unsettled. She felt a great deal of pain but didn't know why. The grandmother went to the yard, opened the door and checked outside. No sign of anyone. She called Tahmooress, "Tahmooress, my dear boy, go see if your uncle has been back. Run to his home and ask if he has any news about your grandfather and Uncle Kaveh. Come, Tahmooress."

The boy rushed out of the room, pulled on his shoes and ran out of the yard. The grandmother pressed her hands together. Now, in the yard, far from her daughter-in-law and granddaughter, she wrung her hands and fidgeted with the edge of her scarf, her face pale and her heart aching. She went upstairs so she could see outside while she was checking on her daughter-in-law, who was sitting in the room on the floor. Rojan, leaning on the pillow, one hand on her big belly, pulled Kajal to herself to cuddle with her but couldn't say a word. The grandmother looked outside but saw no sign of anyone.

Tahmooress arrived at his uncle's house a couple of alleys away. A group of men in their

Kurdish outfits were standing outside but there was no sign of his uncle. One of the men noticed him, whispered something to another man and came towards him. "What are you doing here, dear?" The man knelt beside Tahmooress to be face to face with him, held his little hands in his rough working hands, and asked again with sympathy, "Tahmooress dear, what brings you here, my son?" The man's voice had cracked at the words "my son," but he blinked back the tears so the boy didn't see.

Tahmooress heard a familiar voice from the house. His uncle was screaming, but he couldn't tell if he was angry or in pain. He was scared. His two cousins, the same age as him, in their red Kurdish dresses, were standing frozen at the doorway and staring at him instead of running toward him playfully like always. He didn't run toward them either. With his hands held in the old man's, he stared at his cousins and then looked around at the neighbors' rooftops and windows. The neighbor across the street was staring at his uncle's house. Two old women from the house next door were sitting together on the rooftop.

"Is your mom well, dear? Your grandma? What are you doing here?" the man repeated, and Tahmooress started to talk. "My grandma has sent me to my uncle's house to bring him home. My mom is not well and wants to go to prison to see my dad. She's waiting for her brother, uncle Alimardan, but he hasn't shown up." The man turned his head to his uncle's backyard and said, "Oh, my dear boy, Alimardan is here too, in your uncle's house," and picked the boy up in his arms, against his will, and pressed him to his chest with teary eyes. The boy looked at his cousins, who both ran inside and came back with their mother and two other women, all with eyes puffy from crying. They were all looking inside the house.

The men at the doorstep went inside. The crying sounds of men filled the house. Tahmooress wanted to go inside but the older man was still holding him tightly in his arms. His uncle, Alimardan, came outside. Tahmooress, who felt relieved, called him. His uncle wiped his tears and said, "Yes dear." The boy, now released from the man's open arms, ran towards his uncle. Alimardan hugged him and said, "My little man. My dear. Is your mom home?"

"Yes, she's waiting for you"

"What is it I can do, dear?" Alimardan said, crying.

The other uncle came out of his home, in

a white undershirt and his Kurdish pants, holding a black shirt in his hand and told Alimardan, "You stay here. Your sister needs you. Kaywan and his brother will go after my father and brother." Then he knelt in front of Tahmooress, held his shoulders tightly in his hands and said, "Your father was a real man, my dear child. He was a real man and we weren't, my boy. He was a real man and we weren't. He went lonely." And then he hugged the boy tightly.

A woman ran from the end of the alley towards his aunt and said, "The doctor is on his way. He'll be here shortly."

"Shouldn't we take him to the clinic?" his aunt asked.

"But how?" his uncle said. Then told the other uncle, "Him on one side and your mother on the other side. I wish my mother was still alive." Tahmooress's uncle, still holding him, turned to him and said, "Your father was a real man and died like a real man. Do you understand? He died like a real man," and hugged him tightly again.

A blue truck sidled down the road and stopped in front of the house. The doctor got out from the passenger seat, looked at the people who were all outside now and asked the uncle, "What happened?" The older man who had previously been holding Tahmooress said quietly, "Kaveh and his father went to the city. They had a call from prison saying that he's being released today. These poor souls went there with his clothes and sweets and found out he'd been executed this morning. His father had a heart attack. His wife, who's going to have a baby any minute, is anxious and panicking. Neither she nor his mother know yet." The doctor went back to the car and sat down heavily in the passenger seat, his feet still outside.

Car

There was a traffic jam on the street and no way out of the long line of honking cars. It wasn't clear if the city was celebrating or if it was enraged. In one second, you would feel scared of being on the streets, and in the next second, you would feel brave. In a moment, you would want to scream, and in another, you would drown in a deep silence.

He'd never felt like this until these recent days. It felt like depression had started dancing around. He told himself, "You're depressed. But why is depression reveling in your soul?"

In the car on his right, a fifty-year-old man with a tired face was madly pressing his hand on the steering wheel. The man was honking, but no one could hear it amidst the screams of the crowd and other honking noises around. A middle-aged woman was sitting in the back seat and looking for something or someone with her big eyes.

"So the man should be a cab driver," he thought to himself. "Maybe he's in a rush but he doesn't look angry with the cars in front. It's something else. Same as the woman. She doesn't seem to be in a rush, more like waiting for something." On his left, two twenty-something-year-old girls were in another car. One of them was taking a video with her phone and the other one was checking around, like a bodyguard in the Hollywood movies. They didn't seem in a rush either.

Amongst the big line of cars, hundreds of people on bikes were trying to find gaps, and even people were running everywhere in between. Nothing seemed like before. The crowd was huge but it didn't feel like winning the soccer league. It didn't look like the uprising twelve years ago. Not even like the uprising four years ago. He told himself, "I've been in all those uprisings but this time everything is different. It's like people's beliefs have changed. They live on the streets. They sleep, grow, and die on the streets."

The street always reminded him of a house. The cars were the rooms, and the strangers were the same household. A big family in a big house with many rooms. His windows were up. He checked the radio and noticed it was on but couldn't hear any sound and reached his hand to turn the volume up but it was on the highest. He heard a faint sound of music but didn't understand why he couldn't hear it when the volume was so high. Tried to turn his head but it was hard. He was lightheaded like right before falling asleep. Now he could hear some voices louder but still not clear. Wanted to scream but it felt like sleep paralysis. No sound was coming out of his throat. Asked himself, "Am I dreaming?" But no, he could remember honking in solidarity with the chanting people, on his way home here on Moallem street.

He felt short of breath. It was like there was no oxygen in the air. He was breathing and could feel the flow of air in his nose, mouth, and throat but not the oxygen in his lungs. Didn't feel any exhale, only inhale. Looked at the windshield. It was cracked, and the cracks were growing slowly bit by bit. "When did the windshield break?" He couldn't remember. His feet felt cold. Asked himself, "Are you scared?"

He heard his mother's voice, singing with the sound of the water running, by the kitchen sink: "The carp, covered in mud, emerged from the depths of the marsh." He felt his body was stuck in the pond and his head was out, with his neck hot and his head light. He was sleepy, and wanted to sleep right there in the middle of all the noise and smoke. Couldn't keep his eyes open. It felt like high-school history class on a hot summer day at noon, when his eyes would close and he would open them embarrassed. But it wasn't a summer's day, and he wasn't a teenager. In fact, it was an autumn night and he was already thirty years old. So where was this sunlight coming from?

He could hear a voice very faintly. It sounded like people were screaming and banging on the windows of the cars but he didn't care any more. Just wanted to sleep. He was tired and had been tired for a long time. He had not felt this sleepy ever. Closed his eyes and everything felt calm.

But the world in the cars around him was actually wailing. The two girls in the car on the left were screaming nonstop and hitting themselves in the face and head. The man who had been sitting in the car on the right was now banging on the passenger window with a steering lock, and it shattered. The man, having broken the window, opened the door and and jumped in, reached across to the driver's door. Two young men opened the door. One of them was pressing on the driver's throat to stop the bleeding, while the other one, with shaking hands, was desperately trying to open the seat belt. The car was surrounded by the crowd and the flashes of the cell phone cameras were pointed at the young driver. Someone was screaming, "Those murderers killed him. Those cowards killed him."

Hamed's phone was on his lap, turned on, and on the screen, his wife and mother-in-law were screaming. The young man who opened the driver's seat belt noticed the phone and the video call. He didn't dare to touch the phone. He was scared to pick it up. Hamed's wife was shouting nonstop, 'Hamed! Hamed! Hamed!' Beside her, his mother-in-law was also screaming. The young man instinctively reached for the phone, pushed the red button, and stopped the video call. The screen turned black.

Home

"Wow, Mom, come see what's going on! Hamed, zoom in and show me a closeup. I wish I was there. The hell with this disease that doesn't let me be there in the crowd. Do you know, Hamed, how long I've been waiting for this? Mom, come see. Hamed, do you see any guards around? What if they see you're recording this?"

"Not at all. No sign of guards. Even if there are any, they don't dare to come forward. Hanieh dear, the crowd is so big that even the army won't do anything, never mind a couple of Basij thugs with BB guns and paint guns."

The mother came behind Hanieh and poked her head into the phone screen, joining the video chat. Hamed could see both Hanieh and her mother on the phone, but they saw the view in front of Hamed. "Hi, baby! Oh dear Hamed, be careful. Don't let anything happen to you. You are going to be a father. Your wife is not well. You have so many responsibilities."

Hanieh turned her head around and looked at her and very gently pushed her away with her hand. "Mom, what are you talking about? What responsibility? I myself should have gone with him to the street." Then, placing her right hand on her six-month-pregnant belly, she smiled and said, "This baby is coming to this dog cage with all these filthy thieves to do what? If anything can be done for this baby, it's to have the hospitals free of Mullah's picture when she's being born, to have a lion and sun on the country's flag, and to make her born free like her name, Raha."

Hamed smiled when hearing the name Raha, glanced at his wife's picture on the phone and said, "See Mom, I don't have a normal wife. She is a partisan. No wonder her social-media handle is Partisan with Red Lipstick." He laughed. "Hey, Partisan, why is your lipstick pale today? Are you okay? You need to change your ID to Raha's Mom, you know."

Hanieh answered quickly, "You should have been pregnant with your sensitive soul and I should have been in the streets. What kind of name is Raha's Mom? Hamed, didn't you park the car and walk on the street to see what's happening?"

Hamed turned the phone to himself and

said to the camera, "Do you even see any parking spots? But I got out of the car a couple of times to encourage people to honk. It's very different this time, Hanieh. Old and young people seem to want the same thing. Hijab or no hijab, beard or no beard, they are all on the same side. But I'm still surprised about who these thug oppressors are. Hanieh, you won't believe it but I saw at least ten army guards who looked worried for people and would run towards people and guide them to safety with sign language. I don't know if I'm carried away or if it's true. It's hard to believe that these miserable army guards also don't want people to leave the streets—"

His sentence wasn't finished when there was the sound of glass breaking and the phone fell. Hanieh screamed. The mother ran from the kitchen to Hanieh and the phone. The phone showed the ceiling of the car, a part of Hamed's chest and his yellow T-shirt, which was slowly turning red, and the snorting sound of Hamed's breathing.

Hanieh was squeezing her pregnant belly with both hands like she was pushing a cherry seed out. She kept screaming Hamed's name. The mother didn't know what she was supposed to do. She was holding Hanieh's hand with one hand and pushing on her own chest with the other. She felt like she was going to have a heart attack, like she was about to deliver. She was howling, "Dear Hamed!"

Time had slowed down with the spread of red blood on the yellowness of Hamed's T-shirt, until the video-call connection was abruptly cut.

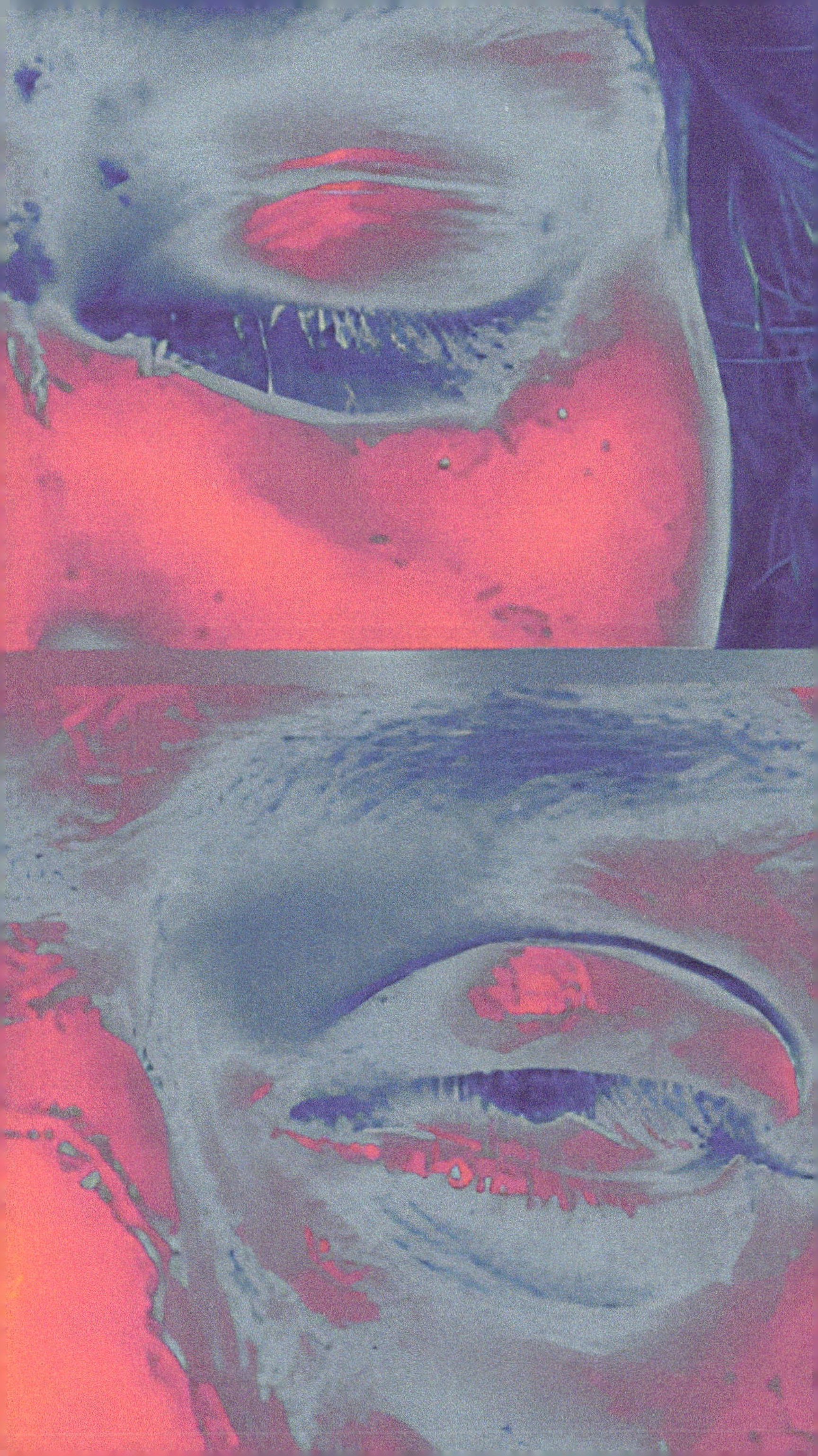

Hospital

The nurse entered the room without knocking, for the first time. A middle-aged physician was sitting behind a desk, and the sudden opening of the door and the night nurse's panicked look astonished him.

"Ms. Riahi!" He couldn't finish his sentence and was cut off by the nurse, who looked like she'd just lost her child.

"Doctor, please come and help. They are gonna take her. Please save her," said the nurse with a sob in her trembling voice. The doctor got off his chair, took his glasses off, left his pen on the desk, took a couple of steps toward the nurse and asked, "What's wrong, Ms. Riahi? Whom are they taking away?"

The young nurse, with a pale face, burst into tears when the doctor got closer. She covered her mouth and nose with her fist, tried to keep her head down to avoid eye contact and said, crying, "They've shot this young girl blind and don't even let us give her painkillers. They want to take her. She's in a really . . ." She couldn't even finish her sentence. The doctor was also in shock. He'd never seen the unit team leader this broken and desperate. She, who could always run the emergency unit so easily, was now so desperate like she'd lost everything. He didn't know whether he should hug her or calm her down, but he had something bigger to take care of.

"Where is she, Ms. Riahi? Let's go."

The nurse rushed out of the room and ran down the hall on the right, the longest one in the hospital, towards the emergency department. The doctor walked fast to catch up with her but couldn't, so he started running. He thought to himself that it wasn't the first time he'd felt this way. A few years ago, he was a resident in Rajaie Hospital, when the Roodbar earthquake victims were transferred. He'd worked two days in a row alongside other staff and doctors. This feeling of running brought back that memory, but he didn't have time to think now. His forehead sweating, he remembered the first limbs he had to amputate with a saw, the fainting of the doctors one by one. No one believed a young new graduate could survive two days of bloodshed and death. His life took a turn that night and he became an emergency doctor.

The nurse turned left, opened two back-to-back doors and entered the emergency department. It looked like a war zone.

"What are these soldiers doing here with their weapons?" An anti-protest soldier in a black uniform, laden with gear, supplies, paintball guns, and shotguns, scanned the crowd. These paintball guns were often used to mark protesters but sometimes loaded with hard bullets meant to injure. Shotguns were used for more severe harm. The authorities frequently used these weapons to injure protesters while deceiving international human rights organizations by claiming no live ammunition was used. They often blamed anti-government partisans for using hunting shotguns to deflect responsibility. The soldier couldn't control the turning of his head and eyes as he tried to locate the emergency staff, who seemed to be lost in the crowd.

Ali, the young physician, was sitting in a corner in his blood-stained uniform, tapping on his forehead with his hands and biting his lips. Three of the nurses were screaming in between the armed men and pushing them away like injured lionesses under hyenas' siege. There were six beds in the department but four of them were empty. The patients were begging in the crowd. An old man with an unshaved and pale face was begging a fat, bearded young man, who was yelling at soldier with wide-open eyes, "Bring him outside. He doesn't need anything." Then yelled, "Saleh, bring him to the car in five minutes." And turned and left through the entrance door.

Behind the door, a crowd of visitors, perhaps twenty or twenty-five, were poking their heads through the opening to see the inside like people in the airport waiting for passengers. Of the two security guards, one was standing by the entrance and the other one was trying to speak with one of the same agents, but you couldn't hear him. Everyone's attention was on one of the beds. The doctor went there. Two young boys, late teens, in black jeans and shirts, were lying on the floor by the bed with their hands tied behind them. One of the guards was pushing his foot on the back of one of them and pushing the nurses and patients away with his hands. The other boy, who looked younger, was lying face down and keeping his eyes closed in fear, like a scared baby bird on the floor stalked by a cat. Both boys had blood on their hands. The boy who was under the guard's foot had blood on his leg from his thigh to his calf. The boy who was under the guard's foot had a severe wound on his leg, stretching from his thigh to his calf. It was a mess of punctures and torn flesh, suggesting a close-range injury inflicted by multiple projectiles. A nurse and two women, with loose scarves and expressions of being overwhelmed, scared, and exhausted from those traumatic moments, were leaning against the bed, trying to block the guards. They screamed so loudly that their screams hurt the doctor's ears. The different noises were mixed to the point that his ears started ringing and he could barely track them. He asked himself, "Where's Riahi?" Since he'd entered the emergency department he hadn't seen her. She'd been ahead of him.

Leila, the young new graduate nurse, was bending down on the other side of the bed and working on a young woman who was lying there's face, using gauze and oxygen peroxide, with obvious nervousness and fear. The doctor got focused in a nanosecond by seeing the patient. The voices became clearer. A hand touched his left shoulder and pulled him back. He turned and noticed a guard who wanted to pull him away. He was very young. Maybe even younger than his son, who was in university. The doctor took the young solider's hand, stared into his eyes, and threw his hand away. The guard was stunned for a second. The doctor wasn't scared of him, and it surprised him.

The doctor shouted, "Move back. What's with this nonsense?" Then raised his voice even higher and said, "Who's responsible for the security in here?"

The nurse said quietly, "Rajabi." The doctor called, "Rajabi!"

Rajabi, a very old and thin-haired man

with a white beard and in his security-guard's uniform, was standing two feet away.

"Yes, Doctor," he said.

"What kind of nonsense is this?" the doctor told him with wide, angry eyes. "Everyone should leave." Rajabi wanted to say something but the doctor yelled, "Everyone leaves but the staff." He yelled at the soldiers with his bulging neck muscles, "Everyone leave!" His scream stopped everyone for a moment. He screamed again, "Call the police! What are these people doing here?" A hideous young boy, hardly twenty years old, with sadistic, somewhat crazed eyes, stepped towards him and said, with a leering grin, "If you have anything to say, speak to us, doctor."

The doctor, checking the boy's hand and his dark fingernails, took two steps toward him and said, "What are you on, lad, to be so nasty?" It was common knowledge, though not officially acknowledged, that anti-riot soldiers were often given drugs like Captagon to make them brutal and violent against protesters. There was also evidence of criminals being hired from prisons and unofficially allowed to smoke crack for the same reasons. The young guard got nervous, and a couple of other guards looked at him first and then at each other. They were surprised, like they'd been caught in a crime. One, who was behind the others, looked down upon hearing the phrase, "What are you on?" and left. The doctor looked into the other guard's eyes and screamed, "I give the orders here! Rajab, kick everyone out!"

The guard who was pushing his foot on the injured boy's back grabbed the back of his shirt neck with two hands and pulled him up to take him out. The doctor held his hand,

"He is injured. The injured people stay. Others leave." The guard released his hand and stepped back. The doctor called out to Riahi, his voice strained with urgency. She was right beside him, but her senses were overwhelmed by the chaos, and she couldn't register his presence. He gave the boy to her and pointed at the bed next to them. He said, "Put him on the bed. Untie his hands first and then lie him down." The nurse and the two women who were guarding the girl's bed moved forward when the guards moved back, like the defense in soccer, making some room.

The doctor noticed the undercover guard who had left the emergency department and was coming back. He screamed, "This is the emergency department and I decide who stays and who leaves. After treatment, anyone can do anything they want behind this door."

He told the undercover guard, "You want to watch? Here, behind the door. There are only two doors. Stay behind the doors."

The guards picked up the boy who was lying on the floor. He looked at the doctor pleadingly. The doctor couldn't see any injuries on him. He suddenly felt really tired. He couldn't even yell any more. He followed the boy's eyes silently until he turned away and was pushed out of the main door. He turned to Leila. Leila was scared.

"What's wrong?" Leila looked at the female patient. She was shocked. It wasn't a woman, but a young girl. She had white, silky skin. Blood ran out from under the gauze that covered her eyes. The doctor lifted the dressing and breathed in once, sharply. Where the girl's eyes had been the sockets were now empty, bloody cavities. Leila cried quietly and, with the gauze soaked in sterile water, cleaned the girl's face. The girl's eyes were shut and she was moaning.

"Dad," she moaned. Leila lifted her head up, looked at the doctor and spoke in a whisper so the girl couldn't hear.

"She's lost her vision. Both her eyes are blinded."

"Dad," the girl said again.

The doctor unconsciously held her right hand in his big hands and said, "Yes dear. Don't worry, my child, we are here right beside you." Leila, stepped back, leaned on the wall and let go of her weight. Her body shaking, the gauze and napkin in one hand, and the sterile water box in the other. The doctor asked Leila kindly, but firmly, "Have you given her sedatives?" Leila shook her head. The doctor called out, "Riahi! give her a sedative!" Riahi was standing right beside him with an IV bag in her hand. Tenderly, the doctor passed the girl's hand to Riahi. Riahi slid the girl's sleeve up. There was a tattoo of three beautiful shorebirds flying on her arm. The doctor leaned over the girl's face and pressed around her eyes very gently with his fingers. It seemed like she didn't feel much pain. He carefully checked here eyes. The eye socket in the right eye was broken, but in the left not. The doctor told Leila, "Call Doctor Manouchehri and ask him to come. Find him wherever he is and tell him I asked him to come. He should be here in any way he can." Leila rushed towards the nursing station in the emergency department. The doctor asked the girl quietly, "What is your name, dear? Do you hear my voice?" The girl didn't reply. The doctor moved closer to her face and asked, "What is your name, my dear child?" The girl turned her head a little to the doctor's voice and said with a broken voice, "Sanaz."

The doctor asked, "How old are you, Sanaz?"

"Sixteen," the girl replied, and the doctor's eyes filled with tears. Riahi had made the sedative ready to mix in the IV bag. The doctor, reaching out with his hand, stopped her, got close to the girl's ear and said, "Sanaz, dear, do you remember your dad's phone number?" The girl nodded. The doctor said, "Tell me, dear, so I can call him and ask him to join you." The girl repeated the number slowly and quietly, and the doctor, checking around to make sure no one was watching, took a piece of paper and a pen from his pocket. Rajabi, the security guard, was standing there in casual clothes. Noticing what was happening, he tapped on the undercover guard's shoulder and showed him something on his phone to distract him.

The doctor wrote down the number and repeated it for the girl to confirm.

"What is your last name?" he asked.

"Abbasi," the girl said. The doctor caressed the girl's cheek with his hand.

"Don't worry, dear. I'm gonna be here until your dad arrives." He took the sedative syringe from Riahi, gave the paper to her and told her quietly, "Go call her dad from my office and put the paper in my desk drawer." Riahi nodded once, turned around slowly and went toward the other door of the emergency department. Sanaz was not calm; she was mumbling and asking for something, her voice filled with confusion and fear. It was as if she was just beginning to feel the pain and grasp that something major was wrong.

The doctor told the girl while injecting the sedative into the IV bag and gently interrupted her.

"Sanaz, dear, calm down. We are here right beside you," he said softly, trying to soothe her. He then added quietly, "Your dad is also on his way." He caressed the girl's face again and repeated, "Calm down. We are right beside you." He turned around to check on the boy who had brought the girl to the hospital.

"More contemptible than those who commit acts of oppression are those who, in the face of such injustice, remain silent and claim that they cannot judge anyone."

– Hirbod Human

Acknowledgments

I extend my heartfelt gratitude to my dear friend Hermes S.K., whose invaluable support and guidance were instrumental in the creation and production of this book. Your wisdom, encouragement, and unwavering belief in this project and in me have been a constant source of strength. Thank you for standing by me every step of the way. I'd also like to thank Stella Rostami, who helped me develop the English version of these stories and to my editor Edward Wall.

About the Author

Hirbod Human, an esteemed Iranian-American writer, filmmaker, and philosopher, was born during the tumultuous Islamic Revolution in Iran. Witnessing the harsh realities of war and political upheaval firsthand, he later fled to the United States, seeking refuge from oppression. Devoted to documenting and sharing the struggles for human rights and social justice, Hirbod has spent years interviewing victims, survivors, and even perpetrators of political violence in Iran. His work aims to shed light on these untold stories and advocate for the voiceless.

www.ingramcontent.com/pod-product-compliance
Lightning Source LLC
Chambersburg PA
CBHW040122150726
48005CB00015B/2331